I Like - Book 1

By Viola & Zaida Stefano

The rights of Viola & Zaida Stefano to be identified as the authors of this work have been asserted by them in accordance with the **Copyright Amendment (Moral Rights) Act 2000**.

All rights reserved. Apart from any use as permitted by the authors & under the **Copyright Act 1968**, no part may be reproduced, copied, scanned, stored in a retrieval system, recorded, or shared, by any means or in any form, without prior written permission from the publisher.

A catalogue record of this book is available from the **National Library of Australia.**

ISBN: 978-0-6456272-5-1

Authors: Viola Stefano & Zaida Stefano
Illustrations, photographs, cover & internal designs: Zaida Stefano

Illustrations copyright © Zaida Stefano 2022
Design copyright © Zaida Stefano 2022
Photographs copyright © Zaida Stefano 2022

Disclaimer: The content presented in this book is meant for educational purposes only. The authors & publisher claim no accountability to any entity or person for any liability, damage, or loss caused or assumed to be caused directly or indirectly as a consequence of the application, use, or interpretation of the material in this book.

VeeZee Publications

Copyright © VeeZee Publications Pty Ltd 2022
First published in Australia in 2022
by VeeZee Publications Pty Ltd
veezeepublications.com

Learning made easy with

VeeZee!

- **Focus Core words in 'I Like - book 1' and the 'I Like' series** (yellow)
- **Secondary Core words in 'I Like - book 1' and the 'I Like' series** (blue)
- **Other secondary Core words in the 'I Like' series but NOT in 'I Like - book 1'** (green)

Core Vocabulary used throughout VeeZee Publications

I	want	can	stop	**look**
like	**more**	**he**	go	see
here	what	**do**	**the**	**and**
out	where	**we**	**it**	**up**
not	**they**	when	**that**	**down**
she	now	them	is	put
help	off	**you**	yes	on
turn	who	**this**	no	why
done	make	a	**to**	under
come	in	some	which	**there**
open	get	good	same	home

All Core word readers through the various ranges in VeeZee Publications have been developed around specific themes. The themed photos and illustrations present a backdrop for the Core words used in each book. Your students are exploring and interpreting the messages conveyed by these images. They are learning to consider the text in order to understand the images. They are therefore making links between images and the corresponding texts. You are using a range of Core words when discussing the photos and illustrations with your students, specifically; who, what, where, when and why. The use of these 'question' words in discussion further reinforces their meanings and their associations with surrounding words. We recommend that students without a vision impairment also explore the readers designed for students with low vision. This will support interaction and discussion amongst the students. It is our hope that this will ultimately promote acceptance, understanding, compassion and teamwork, thus cultivating true inclusion.

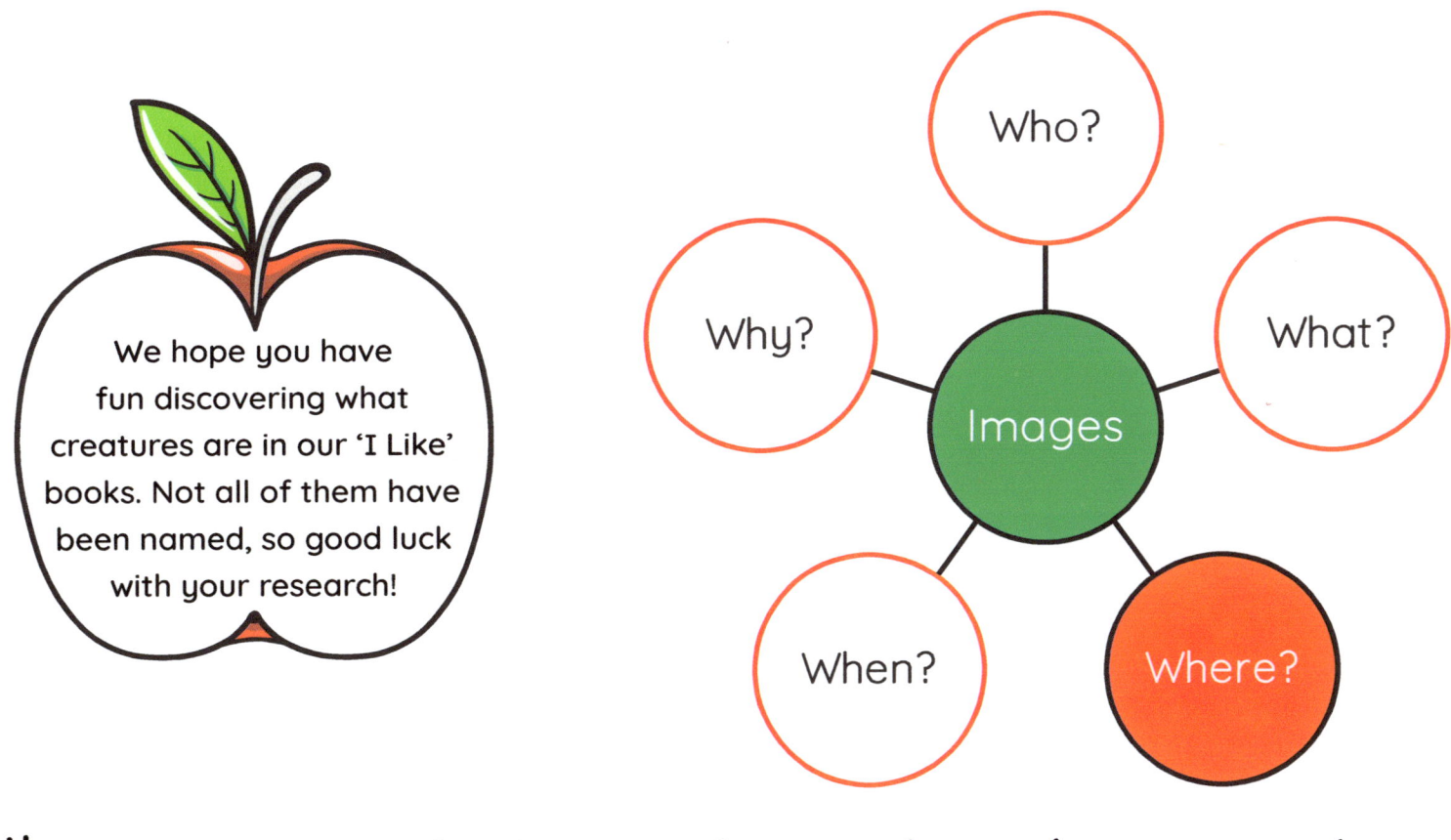

We hope you have fun discovering what creatures are in our 'I Like' books. Not all of them have been named, so good luck with your research!

Where can you find your favourite colour in nature?

I like red.

I like yellow.

I like purple.

He likes orange.

She likes pink.

I like blue.

I like white.

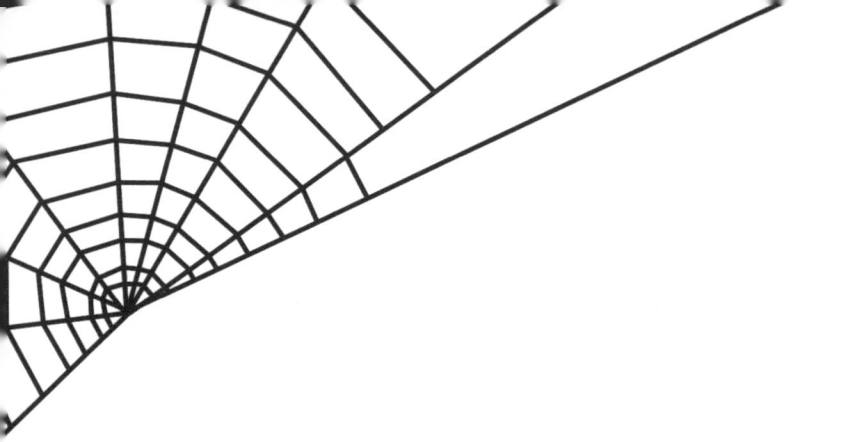

I like the spider.

I like the beetle.

She likes it.

He likes it.

I like the ant.

I like the locust.

He likes bees.

She likes flowers.

I like the flowers.

Words in this book

I	ant	flowers
like	locust	spider
the	bees	beetle
likes	it	

Words in this book

red	yellow	purple
orange	pink	blue
he	white	she

Do you know the focus Core words: 'I' and 'like'? Read the words along each line.						
I	like	like	I	like	like	I
I	like	I	like	like	I	like
like	I	like	I	I	like	I
like	I	I	like	like	I	like
I	like	like	like	I	like	I
like	like	I	like	like	like	like
I	I	like	I	like	I	like

Do you know the focus and secondary Core words in this book (refer to Core word table)? Find them along each line, point to them and say them. Read the other words too once you have pointed to the Core words.

I	the	like	I	red	like	it
like	I	flowers	ant	purple	like	white
the	like	beetle	I	bees	likes	like
I	spider	I	orange	the	blue	like
likes	she	the	like	he	like	I
locust	I	like	like	I	pink	like
I	like	yellow	I	locust	I	like

How many times did you read the word 'I'?
How many times did you read the word 'like'?

Make new words with '_ _ _ _ ike', e.g., 'hike'. Write sentences using these words.

We hope you had fun reading!

VeeZee Publications

Wait, there's more!

Visit our website for information about our range of readers & supporting products.

veezeepublications.com

www.ingramcontent.com/pod-product-compliance
Lightning Source LLC
Chambersburg PA
CBHW050852010526
44107CB00047BA/1582